GrandPa, Tell Me Your Story

*A Grand Father's Guided Journal
and Memory Keepsake Book*

This journal belongs to :

From Your Grand Child :

Copyright © 2023 by Tell it All Press

Hardcover ISBN: 978-1-961443-28-0

All rights reserved. No part of this book may be reproduced, distributed, or transmitted in any form or by any means, including photocopying, recording, or other electronic or mechanical methods, without the prior written permission of the author, except in the case of brief quotations embodied in critical reviews and certain other noncommercial uses permitted by copyright law.
This book is a work of fiction. Any resemblance to actual events, locales, or persons, living or dead, is entirely coincidental.

Published by Harbour House Publishing Press

Printed in the United States of America
Cover design by Victor Oj
Editor and Illustrator: Elsie Bloomfield

Dedicated to my Sons
Valen, vishal & Videl

table of content

01. introduction — 5

02. getting the most out of this journal — 6

03. my detail, time capsule & family tree — 7

04. growing up — 15

05. family heritage — 24

06. career — 37

04. love and relationship — 50

05. parenting — 64

06. health — 73

07. leisure/passion/travelling — 84

08. note to loved ones — 97

introduction

This journal is designed specifically for Grand fathers of all kinds, whether biological or non-biological, to capture and preserve the significant moments that have shaped your life.

GrandPa, Tell Me Your Story™

----GrandPa ----

It's time to write the story of your life with this guided journal.

It's designed to be filled out with an erasable pen or pencil, whichever you prefer.

As you work through the prompts in this journal, you will have the opportunity to record all the important phases of your life, from childhood to elderhood.

You will be able to reflect on your relationships, your achievements, and the challenges you faced. And as you do so, you will be creating a legacy for your grandchildren and future generations to treasure.

In addition to the prompts provided, this journal also includes special pages where you can document your Likes and Dislikes, your travels, Notes to Loved ones, birthdays, special milestones, memories, and more.

We hope this journal will be a source of joy and fulfillment as you document your life story. Let's get writing!

getting the most out of this journal

welcome to this guided journal! It's important to remember that there are no strict rules or guidelines for using this book. **The format is flexible, allowing you to tackle the questions in any order you choose.** Whether you prefer to skip around or work through them in order, the choice is yours.

As you respond to each question, there is no right or wrong way to answer. You may choose to skip certain questions or replace them with additional ones available on our website. It's important to write freely and record whatever comes to mind and heart without overthinking or holding back. The best answers are the ones that come straight from the heart, without worrying about perfection or formality.

Take your time with answering the questions. As there are many of them, you may want to complete the book over multiple sessions, dedicating some time each day over a period of weeks or months. You can also enlist the help of a family member to ask you the questions out loud and record your answers on video or audio.

HINT:
- When telling your story, use specific details such as first and last names, exact dates, locations, and brand names.
- Describing things like "mist-green 1945 Cadillac" instead of "...Dad's Car" and "... red roses" instead of "flowers" helps make your story more vivid.
- Also, be precise, such as "...Schrafft's on seventh Street, downtown," instead of "...at Schrafft's." This approach will bring your story to life and make it more engaging.

If you need more space to answer a question, you can utilize the extra notes pages at the end of each section or include memorable photos. Remember to go easy on yourself and enjoy the process of reflecting on your life experiences.

...my details, time capsule and family tree.

Tell it All Books

chapter 1:
the family tree

This guided journal session is a heartfelt invitation for you to share your incredible life story with your children and grandchildren. The first chapter is all about our Family Tree. The roots, branches, and leaves of our family are unique and valuable, and it is essential that we preserve and cherish these connections.

The Family Tree chapter will delve deep into the origins of our family, allowing you to recount the stories of your parents, grandparents, siblings, and other close relatives. This exercise will help your loved ones learn about their lineage, celebrate the legacy you have created, and foster a deeper sense of belonging. By sharing your memories, experiences, and the lessons you've learned, you will not only enrich the lives of your children and grandchildren but also strengthen the bond between generations.

As you reflect upon your past, take this opportunity to share the joys, the hardships, and the moments that have made you the person you are today.

This chapter will guide you through a series of questions, which will help you share your journey of love, resilience, and growth with your loved ones. As you ponder on the questions, allow yourself to reconnect with your emotions and memories, and let your heart guide you in sharing these precious stories.

We embark on this journey with great love and gratitude, Grandpa. Your stories and wisdom will be cherished and passed down for generations, creating a beautiful and lasting legacy. Thank you for sharing the unique tapestry of our family tree, and may this chapter be the first of many that celebrate your incredible life.

MY DETAILS

Full Name

Place of Birth

Eye Color

Hair Color

Height

time capsule

TODAY'S DATE ....

The Price of...

Gallon of Milk	
Gallon of Gasoline	
Movie Ticket	
Landline Telephone	
Pair of Jeans	
Vinyl Music Album	
Loaf of Bread	
Movie Rental (VHS)	
Fast-Food Meal	
New Car	
Magazine	
Postage Stamp	
Newspaper	
Mortgage Interest Rate	
Monthly Rent/Mortgage Payment	
Average Weekly Wages	
Average House Rate	

FAMILY TREE

Your Great Grandmother

Your Great Grandfather

Your Great Grandmother

Your Great Grandfather

Your Grandmother

Your Grandfather

Your Father

Your Brothers

You

FAMILY TREE

Your Great Grandmother

Your Great Grandfather

Your Great Grandmother

Your Great Grandfather

Your Grandmother

Your Grandfather

Your Mother

Your Sisters

YOUR FAVOURITE.......

Color	Number

Flower	Animal

Films	Actors

Songs	Musicians

Books	Authors

Seasons	Country

TV Series	Weather

getting to know you more...

Food:

Drink:

Color:

Hobby:

Song:

Show:

Games:

App:

City:

Country:

...growing up

Tell it All Books

Chapter 2:
growing up

This is a crucial part of your legacy, as it is here that we explore the foundation of who you are today. Your children and grandchildren will cherish the opportunity to learn about your roots and understand the experiences that shaped you during your formative years.

In this chapter, we will dive into the emotions, memories, and moments that defined your childhood and adolescence. From the home you grew up in, to the neighborhood where you played with friends, we want to capture the essence of your early years. Think back to the people who influenced you, the lessons you learned, and the dreams you had as a young person.

By sharing these experiences, you are not only preserving your own memories, but also creating an invaluable gift for your family. This exercise serves as a bridge between generations, fostering a deeper connection and understanding between you and your loved ones. Through your words and emotions, they will walk in your footsteps, see the world through your eyes, and appreciate the journey you have taken.

As you answer the questions in this chapter, remember that every detail matters. Your story is unique, and even the smallest memory may hold great significance for those who come after you. As you reminisce, let the emotions flow, and don't be afraid to express joy, sadness, or any other feelings that emerge. This will make your narrative even more authentic and relatable.

By delving into these questions and more, we will create a vivid and heartfelt account of your early years. Your story is a treasure, Grandpa, and we are honored to help you share it with generations to come.

this or that

extravert	introvert
books	movies
art	sport
burger	pizza
juice	soda
dark	light
academia	academia
dogs	cats

Tell it All Books

Growing Up

When and where were you born?

Where did you grow up?

Growing Up

What was it like?

How would you describe yourself as a child? Were you happy?

Growing Up

What is one of your best memories of childhood? Worst?

Did you have a nickname? How'd you get it?

Growing Up

Do you have any favorite stories from your childhood?

....
....
....
....
....
....
....
....
....
....

When you were a child, what did you want to be when you grew up?

....
....
....
....
....
....
....

Other Things

Other Things

...family heritage

this or that

Coffee	Tea
Chesee Cake	Cupcake
Mounth	Beach
Pizza	Burger
Paris	Hawai
Flat Shoes	Casual Shoes
Hot	Ice
Cooking	Reading
Music	Karaoke

Chapter 3:
Family Heritage

It's with deep love and admiration that I invite you to embark on this journey with us. We are here to discover and preserve the stories and memories that have shaped our family heritage. This chapter is dedicated to the roots of our story, the foundation from which our family tree has blossomed.

Your children and grandchildren are eager to learn about the origins of our family, the traditions we've inherited, and the values we hold dear. By sharing your memories and experiences, you're not only helping us understand where we come from, but also contributing to the richness and depth of our family's history.

This exercise will provide a space for you to reminisce, reflect, and share the stories that have shaped your life.

It is through these stories that we can continue to pass down the wisdom and lessons you've learned, keeping our family's legacy alive for generations to come.

We want to capture the essence of our family's heritage, to hold onto the moments and memories that have brought us to where we are today. This journey will not only strengthen our connections with each other but also create a precious treasure for future generations to cherish.

So, dear Grandpa, we hope you'll join us in this heartfelt endeavor to preserve our family's history. Your stories are invaluable, and we're eager to learn from your experiences and wisdom. Together, let's weave the tapestry of our family's past, to celebrate and honor the roots of our story.

Family

Who were your parents?

What were your parents like?

Family

How was your relationship with your parents?

Do you have any siblings? What were they like growing up?

Family

Who were your favorite relatives?

Do you remember any of the stories your grandparents used to tell you?

Family

How did you and grandma/grandpa meet?

Do you remember any songs that you used to sing to your children?

Family

Were your grandparents well-behaved?

What were your parents like?

What were your grandparents like?

FAMILY HERITAGE

Where are your parents' families from?

Have you ever been there? What was that experience like?

FAMILY HERITAGE

What traditions have been passed down in your family?

....
....
....
....
....
....
....
....
....
....

Do you remember any traditional story about your family?

....
....
....
....
....
....
....
....

FAMILY HERITAGE

What are the classic family stories? Jokes? Songs?

Do you remember any traditional story about your family?

Other Things

Other Things

...career

Tell it All Books

Chapter 4:
career

As you've traveled the winding roads of life, you've experienced countless moments that have shaped who you are today. Your career has played a significant role in your life's journey and holds a wealth of memories and lessons for future generations to cherish. This chapter, "The Path of a Lifetime - Your Career Journey," aims to capture the essence of your professional life, highlighting the achievements, challenges, and wisdom you've gained along the way.

This exercise is a priceless opportunity for your children and grandchildren to walk in your footsteps, understanding how your career has molded you into the person they admire today. Through your stories, they'll gain insight into the decisions you made, the obstacles you overcame, and the values that guided you throughout your working life.

By sharing your experiences, you're giving them a unique perspective on history, as well as invaluable advice that may one day help them navigate their own career paths.

This journey of self-discovery will also serve as a poignant reminder of the resilience, passion, and determination you've shown throughout your professional life.

To embark on this meaningful adventure, we'll start by exploring the origins of your career aspirations, tracing your steps as you ventured into the working world, and delving into the most memorable moments that shaped your professional identity. As you answer the questions in this chapter, remember that your honest and heartfelt responses will make this a truly cherished keepsake for your loved ones.

This or That

WEEKEND ACTIVITIES

Read books	Listen to a podcast
Cook food	Order in
Wake up early	Wake up late
Sleep early	Sleep late
Alone time	Family time
Learn a new dish	Learn a new skill
Do chores	Declutter
Workout	Relax
Movie marathon	TV series binge watching

School

Did you enjoy school?

What kind of student were you?

What would you do for fun?

School

How would your classmates remember you?

Are you still friends with anyone from that time in your life?

What are your best memories of grade school/high school/college/graduate school?

School

Worst memories? ....
....
....
....
....
....
....
....
....

Was there a teacher or teachers who had a particularly strong influence on your life? Tell me about them.
....
....
....
....
....
....
....
....
....

Career

Describe the work that you do.

Tell me about how you got into your line of work.

Career

Do you like your job? ....

....
....
....
....
....
....
....
....
....
....

What did you think you were going to be when you grew up? ....

....
....
....
....
....
....
....
....
....

Career

What did you want to be when you grew up?

What lessons has your work life taught you?

Career

If you could do anything now, what would you do? Why?

Do you plan on retiring? If so, when? How do you feel about it?

Career

Do you have any favorite stories from your work life? ....

....
....
....
....
....
....
....
....
....
....
....
....
....
....
....
....
....
....
....
....
....
....
....

Other Things

Other Things

...love and relationship

Tell it All Books

this or that

Forest	Mountain
America	Europe
Summer	Winter
Pack Light	Overpack
Local food	Fancy reSto
Glamping	Camping
Hotel	Airbnb
Small town	City life

Chapter 5:
love and relationship

As your **children and grandchildren**, we yearn to know more about the special connections that have been a cornerstone of your existence. This exercise serves as a precious opportunity for us to not only deepen our understanding of you but also to cherish and celebrate the love that has touched your life.

It's essential for us to hear your stories, as they hold the key to understanding the love and compassion that reside within our family. From your first love to the moment you met Grandma, from friendships that have stood the test of time to the bonds that have strengthened you in times of need, we want to know it all. By sharing these intimate stories, you will be imparting valuable lessons on love, commitment, and the importance of nurturing relationships, which will undoubtedly impact future generations.

The **questions in this chapter are designed** to help you reminisce about your past, explore the emotions that have accompanied your relationships, and reflect on the meaningful experiences that have made you the person you are today. As you delve into these memories, you may find yourself rekindling old feelings, re-experiencing moments of joy, and even confronting instances of sorrow. Rest assured, this is a safe space for you to share your heart's truth with us.

Your willingness to participate in this exercise not only enriches our family's history but also allows us to honor your legacy, fortify our bonds, and appreciate the love and sacrifices you've made throughout your life. Your memories will serve as an everlasting testament to the love and relationships that have shaped your world and ours.

Friendships

Who Was you best friend? ....

....
....
....
....
....
....
....

What was your first memory of your best friend ....

....
....
....
....
....
....
....
....
....
....
....

Friendships

What things makes such good friends?

How would you describe your friends?

Friendships

How would you describe yourself to your friends?
....
....
....
....
....
....
....
....

What is the presents situation of friendships
....
....
....
....
....

How frequently do you communicate with your friends?
....
....
....
....
....

Love & Relationships

Do you have a love of your life?

When did you first fall in love?

Can you tell me about your first kiss?

Love & Relationships

What was your first serious relationship?

Do you ever think about previous lovers?

What lessons have you learned from your relationships?

Love & Relationships

Who were the "ones that got away" in your life?

What was the hardest break up you've ever experienced?

Do you remember the best date you ever went on?

Marriage & Partnership

How did you meet your spouse/partner?
....
....
....
....
....
....
....
....
....

How did you know they were "the one"?
....
....
....
....
....

How did you propose?
....
....
....
....
....

Marriage & Partnership

What were the best times?

The most difficult times?

Marriage & Partnership

What advice do you have for young couples?

Do you have any favorite stories from your marriage or about your partner?

Other Things

Other Things

...parenting

Tell it All Books

this or that

sunrise	sunset
sweet	savory
sun	moon
early bird	night owl
take a risk	just relax
park	beach
family time	me time
bar	cafe
diy	buy
tv series	movies

Chapter 6: parenting

This is a time for you to reminisce about the joys and challenges of raising your children, and the wisdom you've gathered along the way. By exploring these memories, you will not only connect with your own experiences, but also leave a lasting legacy for your children, grandchildren, and future generations.

This exercise is vital for several reasons. Firstly, it allows your family to learn about your unique parenting style and the principles that guided your decisions. This will provide them with valuable insights into the family's history, and the values that have shaped their own lives. Secondly, this reflection gives you a chance to revisit cherished moments with your children, as well as acknowledge the lessons you've learned from the struggles you've faced.

Take your time and delve into the memories of your parenting journey. Were there any milestones that filled you with pride or moments that tugged at your heartstrings? What challenges did you overcome, and what support systems helped you along the way? As you answer these questions, remember that your stories will serve as a beacon for your loved ones, guiding them through their own parenting journeys and strengthening the bond between generations.

In this chapter, embrace the emotions that come with being a parent - the love, the fear, the joy, and the sorrow. Your vulnerability and honesty will be a testament to the depth of your character, and a priceless gift for those who carry your legacy forward. So, let's embark on this emotional and fulfilling exploration of your parenting journey together, knowing that your experiences will forever be cherished by those who come after you.

Parenting

When did you first find out that you'd be a parent? How did you feel?

Did you always know you wanted to be a parent?

Parenting

Can you describe the moment when you saw your child for the first time?

How has being a parent changed you?

Parenting

What have you learned about yourself from being a parent?

What are your dreams for your children?

Parenting

Do you remember when your last child left home for good?

....
....
....
....
....
....
....
....
....

Do you have any favorite stories about your kids?

....
....
....
....
....
....
....
....

Other Things

Other Things

...health & religion

Tell it All Books

Chapter 7:
Health

As your children and grandchildren, we want to understand your experiences, the battles you've faced, the triumphs you've celebrated, and how your health has shaped you over the years. Our goal is to learn from your wisdom, strength, and resilience, and to see how the choices you made have impacted your wellbeing.

By sharing your story, you're not only preserving a precious part of our family history, but you're also providing us with valuable insights on how we can take care of ourselves and our loved ones. Your experiences will be a guiding light for generations to come.

As you delve into this chapter, remember that health is a deeply personal and emotional topic. We encourage you to be open and honest about your feelings, challenges, and accomplishments. Reflect on how your physical, mental, and emotional wellbeing have evolved over the years, and what lessons you've learned along the way.

Consider discussing key moments in your life, such as:

1. Childhood health
2. Major health events
3. Emotional wellbeing
4. Lifestyle choices
5. Family health history
6. Aging gracefully

By sharing your health journey, you're creating a priceless gift for your family - a testament to the power of perseverance, self-care, and love. We hope that exploring this chapter will not only help you reflect on your experiences but also provide an opportunity for healing, growth, and connection with your loved ones.

this or that

Sport Edition

Aquatic	Golf
Archery	Gymnastics
Badminton	Football
Basketball	Pentathlon
Boxing	Table tennis
Taekwondo	Bicycle
Weightlifting	Volleyball
Long jump	Tennis

Religion

What is your religion?

Can you tell me about your religious beliefs/spiritual beliefs?

Religion

How did you come to your faith?

How has your faith evolved over time?

Religion

What was the most profound spiritual moment of your life?

Do you believe in God?

Religion

How have you experienced God (or a Higher Power) in your life?

Do you believe in the after-life? What do you think it will be like?

Serious Illness

Can you tell me about your illness?

Do you think about dying? Are you scared?

Serious Illness

Has this illness changed you?

What have you learned?

Other Things

Other Things

...Leisure/
Passion/
travelling

this or that

Fashion Edition

Shoe	Shirt
Culottes	Hat
Skirt	Jacket
Jeans	Hoodie
Long Dress	Sweater
pajamas	Blouse
Tunic	Flatshoes
Blouse	Headband

Chapter 8: Travelling/leisure/passion

Travelling is not just about exploring new places, but also about the people we meet, the connections we make, and the lessons we learn along the way. By sharing your experiences, you'll be leaving a precious legacy for your children and grandchildren, allowing them to understand the world through your eyes and heart.

As you share your stories, you'll be gifting your loved ones with a deeper understanding of your life and the world, and inspiring them to embark on their own journeys of discovery. To begin, we'd love for you to share a story about a place that has left an indelible mark on your soul – a destination that moved you, changed your perspective, or ignited your curiosity.

Next, we'll dive into the relationships that enriched your travels. Share stories of the people you met, the friendships you formed, and the unique cultural exchanges you experienced. We're eager to learn about the love and kindness you encountered, as well as the challenges you faced and overcame.

Finally, we'll explore the impact of your travels on your life. How have your journeys shaped your values, your beliefs, and your understanding of the world? What lessons do you hope to pass on to your children and grandchildren, and how can they carry your adventurous spirit with them as they navigate their own paths?

Also your children and grandchildren are eager to learn about the hobbies, interests, and pastimes that have brought you happiness and fulfillment. We understand that these activities may have evolved over time, and we want you to share how they've influenced your life and the person you've become. This chapter will help us bond through shared experiences and inspire us with your unique story.

As you reminisce about the things you loved doing in your leisure time, we want to feel the excitement and enthusiasm you experienced. Whether it was a favorite sport, a creative pursuit, or a simple walk in nature, we want to understand the emotions that were intertwined with these activities.

Take your time to express how these passions have shaped your character, taught you valuable lessons, and left an indelible mark on your soul. The love and dedication you've poured into your interests will serve as an inspiration for us all.

By sharing your story, you're not only creating a lasting legacy for future generations but also giving yourself a chance to reflect on your life, celebrating the moments that have brought you joy and satisfaction. This exercise is a precious opportunity for self-discovery and a gift that will allow us to connect with you on a deeper level.

We eagerly await the stories you'll share in the "Leisure and Passion" chapter, and we're grateful for the opportunity to learn more about the person who has inspired and loved us throughout our lives.

Favorite Things

What is your favorite color?

What is your favorite season?

Favorite Things

What is your favorite car to drive?

What is your favorite book?

Favorite Things

What is your favorite moment in history?
....
....
....
....
....
....
....

What is your favorite perfume/cologne scent?
....
....
....
....
....
....
....
....
....
....
....

Traveling

What is your favorite country to travel to?
....
....
....
....
....
....
....
....
....

What is your favorite continent to travel to?
....
....
....
....
....
....
....
....
....

Traveling

What is your favorite vacation that you have ever been on?

....
....
....
....
....
....
....
....
....

What is your favorite picture taken on vacation?

....
....
....
....
....
....
....
....
....

Traveling

Who is your favorite person to travel with?

What is your favorite thing to bring with you when traveling?

Traveling

What is your favorite food that you have had while on vacation?

....
....
....
....
....
....
....
....
....
....
....
....
....
....
....
....
....
....
....
....

Other Things

Other Things

...note to loved ones

Tell it All Books

this or that

Cat person	Dog person
Jeans	Cullotes
Bright color	Neutral color
Music	Movie
Text	Phone call
Early bird	Night owl
Work out	Watch tv
Staying in	Going out

Note to Loved Ones

Note to Loved Ones

Note to Loved Ones

Note to Loved Ones

Note to Loved Ones

Note to Loved Ones

conclusion

   Throughout our guided journal sessions, we have embarked on a remarkable journey, exploring the rich tapestry of your life's experiences, emotions, and wisdom. As we move towards the conclusion of this heartfelt endeavor, I want to encourage you, with all my heart, not to hold back. Your story, in all its depth and detail, is a priceless treasure that will become our keepsake for years to come.

Each chapter we've traversed has revealed a new facet of your incredible life, providing invaluable insight into your thoughts, feelings, and the experiences that have shaped you. By sharing your story with openness and vulnerability, you have given us the profound gift of understanding the person you truly are. Your resilience, passion, and love have been illuminated, and we can't express how much this means to us.

As we cherish this opportunity to connect with you on a deeper level, I urge you to reveal your heart and soul in these pages. Whether it's the laughter, the tears, or the moments of quiet reflection, every aspect of your life is a treasure that we long to share and celebrate. Your story is not just a collection of memories and moments; it is a testament to the remarkable person you are, and it will serve as an endless source of inspiration, guidance, and love for generations to come.

   ATogether, let's create a lasting legacy, a timeless keepsake that will resonate within the hearts of our family for years to come. Thank you for your courage, your vulnerability, and your willingness to share your story with us. We love you, and we can't wait to learn even more about the amazing person you are.

Notes

Notes

Notes

Notes

GET THIS BOOK
FREE NOW

⟶

Scan This Code
or Visit >>

bit.ly/Einkling

www.ingramcontent.com/pod-product-compliance
Lightning Source LLC
Chambersburg PA
CBHW060407010526
44107CB00005B/615